C000060768

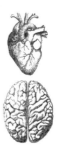

THE NO YOU NEVER LISTENED TO
Meggie Royer

WORDS DANCE PUBLISHING
WordsDance.com

Copyright © Meggie Royer 2015

No part of this book may be used or performed without written consent from the author except for in critical articles & reviews.

1st Edition
ISBN-13: 978-0692463635
ISBN-10: 0692463631

Cover illustration by Christina Mrozik & Zoe Keller
Cover design & interior layout by Amanda Oaks
Editing & proofread by Amanda Oaks

Type set in Bergamo & Strangelove

Words Dance Publishing
WordsDance.com

TRIGGER WARNING

Please be aware that this poetry collection contains art and writing that is potentially triggering. Unfortunately, this is the nature of trauma, though I wish it weren't so. Please take care of yourselves as you read through this book. Stay safe and in a comfortable place, and always, always make sure to take a break if need be.

It's important to note that this collection contains my personal experiences with sexual assault as a survivor. I will have different experiences than you, and some of you may not have any experiences with sexual assault at all- maybe you are reading this out of curiosity, or because you have a friend, relative, or loved one who is a survivor of sexual assault. Please be aware that I will have different experiences, and different responses to these experiences. But never, ever let this cause you to think that your experiences or responses are invalid. They are all valid.

Sending love to everyone who reads this. I hope this collection provides you with some sort of healing. You're worth it. And things will get better.

Dedicated to A, the bravest person I know.
I will love you for as long as I live.

To all the survivors: it wasn't your fault.

THE NO YOU NEVER LISTENED TO

Meggie Royer

❦

THE NO YOU NEVER LISTENED TO

A woman's first blood
doesn't come from between her legs
but from biting her tongue.

AFTERMATH

The moments after. The confusion, the walk back to your house in the dark, the disbelief, the shock. The wreckage, all the friends telling you not to shower in order to keep the evidence intact. The way the ship turns into the shipwreck and everything is drowning, and keeping your head above water seems impossible.

DAUGHTER

Duende, noun, a spirit, fairy, ghost-like creature
Aubade, noun, a song or love poem greeting the dawn.
Afterwards. In my apartment living room
with a single candle on the pillow, still wearing
the same clothes, I pick up the cordless phone
and try to call my mother to tell her what happened.
When she answers, all the most beautiful words I know
come tumbling out instead. The two at the top of this poem.
Sestina, hymnal, equinox. She listens patiently;
I am one of her two daughters, born leap years after the first-
she knows I take my sweet time.
Wernicke's Aphasia. Damage to the brain
that causes one to speak fluently
but meaninglessly. My tongue turns itself inside out
like seafoam. I talk about filling envelopes with grilled cheese
birds driving seashells, mountains opening potholes.
I do not know
how to turn this into a language she will understand.
The word assault is a fish at the end of a very long line
hooking itself deep into an ocean
somewhere on the other side of the equator.

AN ENTIRE COURSE ON EVOLUTION TAUGHT BY A SINGLE SURVIVOR

This is what I want the audience of this poem to know:
       I was inside his bed for a long, long time
       the way black bears hibernate in winter
       and when I left I took all the people I could have been
       before he forced my body onto his
       with me.
Scientists doubt that Eve enjoyed
being reincarnated from Adam's rib
Scientists don't know how to explain
how birds can swallow wedding rings
and their flight is left unaffected.
       I went home to my kitchen and baked
       a dozen loaves of sourdough bread,
       kneaded like it was needed, like kneading
       could punch out the sorrow.
       There was nothing I wanted but to swallow the rage
       like mourning doves do with wedding rings
       and return to living as normal
       with the wings I had before.
There is something else I want the audience of this poem to know:
       the bread burnt.
       I couldn't swallow the rage.
       I took a shower even though all the cop shows advise not to
       because it destroys the evidence.
I think this string of heartbeats that pulses out of sync
and ties itself into a noose
every time I walk past his neighborhood
is evidence enough.

BLUEPRINTS FOR MAPPING OUT A SAD BODY

Back in my own bathroom I dissect myself before the mirror.
Heart appears to still be lodged firmly inside chest,
lungs working correctly, pulse stuttering like Morse code
but still intact. The skin is a different story,
an entirely new novel in which the protagonist hates herself.
Neck covered in blackberry hickeys, bite marks on wrist
like a bracelet of molars, cut lip, thumb-shaped bruise
on left breast. Thumb pressing into a soft apricot.
The anatomist in me shies away from that hidden land
between my legs that was occupied with force.
I do not want to see that part of me
because it will make everything true. Then again,
if there are no bullet holes,
maybe I can convince myself
I wasn't shot.

SUMMER 2014

The neighbors all think I'm preparing for the impending storm.
Loft my bed and carry it outside into the wind,
anchor it deep into the hill like a space observatory.
All my candles are here, my stockpiles of incense, a mason jar of salt
to keep the bad spirits away, a flashlight for undercover reading.
The neighbors all think I'm readying for the flood
that will sweep my house upside down and into the sea
when really I'm practicing for another kind of survival–
the bed is in plain sight of everyone in this town.
If anything happens beneath the covers that shouldn't,
someone will notice.
Someone will call for help
Someone will rescue me this time.

THE CONDUCTOR

There is this at least:
    when I tell all the men in my life whom I love
    about what happened the other night
    most of them ask before hugging
    some of them boil tea for me and read poems aloud
    until my eyelids fill with sand for sleep.
    They all promise they would never do what he did
    to another woman.
This is a promise I hope they can keep.
When my grandfather married my grandmother,
instead of a wedding ring
he handed her an apricot, soft and whole.
Vowed to handle her gently,
to always keep her buried heart safe, like the apricot's pit.
There is this at least:
    that was a promise he kept.
    Now in the octaves of grief that play up and down my spine
    I hope that all these men will spare their loved ones
    this kind of terrible music.

RECIPE FOR BLACKING OUT WHEN YOU FINALLY ESCAPE

After I stumbled home sore:
I told my best friend and we laid on the floor together
held hands while drinking vodka straight from each other's palms.
This would be the part in the movie where the lead actress
can't stop flashing back to the lead actor's mouth
and how he forced her legs apart.
Instead, this is when I get so drunk I pass out,
the entire core of me shaken, not *core* like the inside of the earth
but like the innermost part of an apple
when everything around it has been devoured.
There's too much salt in my mouth
but I didn't swallow the ocean.
My best friend knows what I swallowed.
This is why we're getting drunk.
There is no recipe to handle a disaster like this
without one of the ingredients being hard liquor.

WHEN YOUR FRIENDS ASK ABOUT THE TRAUMA FROM LAST NIGHT LIKE IT'S JUST A BOYFRIEND WHO WENT OUT OF TOWN FOR AN EXTENDED STAY AT A SAD HOTEL

But it's not a boyfriend and it's not something you've learned to love, and if it were a boyfriend it would keep showing up at your doorstep despite all the times you've asked it to leave you alone and never touch you again, it's your heart trying to detach its own lifeline and turn off its own pulse. You watching your best self, the self that holds it all together in front of everyone else, watching that self reach the end of its rope and tie a noose in it.

And you don't want to go to parties anymore but sometimes you do just to lose yourself in drinks and a crowd of people so dense they envelop you like a forest. You remember the tale of Hansel and Gretel, the one you loved as a child and reread over and over again, how there were bread crumbs left between the trees as a trail to remind them how to get back home again, but with trauma there is no home, there is no safe place, there is no returning to anywhere but the place where he shoved you back against the wall and thought his tongue in your mouth was a good thing. But it only prevented you from screaming and now you can only scream on paper and strangers are the only ones who hear your scream and translate it into evergreen trees and salt and longing and mountains and they understand, but the only person you need to understand most is the one who didn't understand at all.

And fuck polygraphs too. They're not proven to work but fuck them anyway. If you were subjected to one you'd say you still love him anyway despite what he did to you and it would register your pulse and your heartbeat as telling the truth but you don't want to hear this truth, you don't want to believe this is the truth, you don't want to believe that you still love the person who caused the trauma, you're in a relationship with trauma and it's complicated.

Volcanoes, monarch butterflies, moondust, spinning salt into sugar and bronze into gold, you have to hold on to all these things and hold them up as examples of destruction but creation at the same time, you feel butterflies in the pit of your stomach whenever you start having sex with strangers, but they say men are from Mars and women are from Venus but you don't want to be from any planet at all when you think of your trauma, you want to be nonexistent, fuck the solar system for telling you that you need to come from Earth and have your origins there, you want to come from a place that doesn't tolerate what happened to you and won't let it ever happen again. In short you want to time travel until you reach a place that doesn't hurt. Birth hurts because it involves blood and guts and you're sick and tired of spilling your guts for strangers that don't have a care in the world about what happens to you.

Your friends ask about trauma like it's just a boyfriend who went out of town for an extended stay at a sad hotel and the only true thing about all this is that it's sad, it's more than sad, it's seeing an entire night sky and Northern Lights and not being able to appreciate a single thing about them other than the fact that the shooting stars remind you of pulling a trigger and trauma is triggering and there is some beauty in language and analogies after all.

BINGE EATING

When the cops question me a week later,
I want to gather one of them up
and kiss him so hard his back cracks,
devour plum after plum after plum, a dozen eggs,
three juiceboxes, as many spoonfuls of mustard
as I can get my hands on,
anything to fill the sinkhole inside my belly
that's been empty ever since the assault.
They ask me if I have any proof of the crime.
I want to hand one of them my aching heart
in a sealed Ziploc bag,
tell them, *take this as evidence*
so I don't have to deal with it anymore
but instead the hunger inside me grows
as the female cop instructs me to undress in front of her
so she can photograph the bruises.

WHAT THE MEN SAID TO ME BEFOREHAND

You have nothing. We will make you whole.
Put away your keys; they won't protect you. This parking lot
is dark for one reason and one reason only. Listen: our hands
will light everything up.
Didn't you know? Your body always comes with strings attached.
We're here to take advantage of them.
Give me a kiss. Come on, use some tongue. Get us warmed up.
I will pull you out of your skin like an anchor.
Why the heavy heart? You knew this was guaranteed.
It's all part of the insurance policy that a woman is born with.
Be still. Be quiet enough that we can hear the cicadas
rubbing against one another, and we won't have to cover your mouth.
You're struggling. Listen, even our hearts weigh ten times
as much as yours. If your heart is a station wagon, our hearts
are Mack trucks. We will run you over and then
come back again for a second helping.
I can almost taste you.
Afterwards, you'll replay this moment over and over again in your head
so often you'll forget the difference between what we did to you
and your favorite song on repeat.
You look like someone who likes it rough.
What, you thought you'd find love? Honey, this is love.
We just have a different way of showing it.
Tonight is the best night for doing this since there's no moon, no stars.
The darkness will cover everything up. It will erase us like ghosts.
The blood will only make you stronger. You already bleed each month
anyway; more blood will change nothing.
Shh. Be still. Don't pretend you didn't know this would happen someday.
We don't have any excuses.
We don't need any.

GODDESS COMPLEX

Persephone, Venus, Athena, all built from fire
with tongues like lightning,
bodies full of warfare and bullet holes.
This is not how I feel, me with this coward heart,
this jumping at touch, the longing for soft skin but the fear
it will eventually hurt me.
My pain will not bridge the River Styx
or launch the sun into the sky,
it will not build temples or make stunning echoes.
Instead, I wake up gasping, covered in salt and sweat,
ribs aching for breath like a fish out of water;
this pain is not beautiful, I am no goddess
who can deal with this and make it powerful,
instead I sit in this bed without wings
and wonder why this happened, how it happened,
and if I could have stopped it.

GUILT

Sometimes even your blood blames you. And sometimes you let it, and you don't know why. There's a whole litany of things you come up with that you could have done differently in order to prevent what happened to you. But that's hindsight bias. That's the untruth. That's like saying you deserved to get shot because you couldn't dodge the bullet in time. Actually, that's like saying you helped pull the trigger. And you didn't.

WHEN MY DAUGHTER SAYS IT WAS HER FAULT

When my daughter tells me the rape was her fault, I will
take her tears and mix them into the smelling salts
that will wake her up whenever she wants to die.
I will teach her the ways of the California Gold Rush:
will tell her that when a boy kneels between her legs without asking
and tries to pan for the prize that will make him rich,
he is only worth coal. Not even bronze.
There will be days when her blood curdles
at the sight of a couple kissing,
when all she wants is to wander through the local cemeteries
in search of the person she used to be
before he buried her beneath his body.
There will be days when forgiveness is a forest
that she has no idea how to find her way through,
when only bread crumbs will signal the path to escape.
And when my daughter says the rape was her fault,
I will gather every last crumb of her dignity
and watch as the wolves of the forest
snarl and snap at its smell.
My daughter will stand and beat her chest,
she will howl and prance
until even the monsters beneath her bed
learn to bow down to her
before they begin to dance.

POLTERGEIST

My ghost is at it again.
Tiptoeing across the floorboards of my house lighting candles
until the melted wax kisses the soles of her feet
and sends smoke up her spine.
Ghosts have no feeling; there are no third-degree burns
This is why every night I catch her fucking a new man
watching me as he explores her mouth with his tongue
like, *This is how you do it properly with men,*
if you had followed my instructions three months ago
you wouldn't have gotten hurt.
She wants to bake me a cake when I learn how to have sex right.
She'll let me stick my fingers in the mixing bowl and lick the spoon
grab fistfuls of angel food and frosting with my bare hands
gorge on the sweetness until my belly expands
to twice its normal size.
This will be our celebration. She'll ask for my autograph.
When I sign my name across her ribcage she'll congratulate me
on having learned my lesson. On not kissing men
unless I'm planning to go all the way.
My ghost is a church with no doors and a bell tolling,
a cornfield I want to get lost in, a shipwreck in disguise.
I can't decide whether to love her or loathe her;
I carry guilt in the bottom of my stomach like a peach pit
and there is nothing more she wants
than to water it and watch it grow.

MISSING PERSON'S REPORT

In the news, a woman is found living with the bodies of her three dead children. On the day of my birth, the nurses taught me the language of apologies first, long before learning how to say *Mamma* or *Dada*. Years later, I say sorry before telling anyone about the rapes. They are all just skeletons in my closet without teeth, because survivors, I was told over and over again, don't have the right to speak.

Anyone could tell the mother of three was unfit for trial. There were black holes in her eyes, a ladder of thorns where her spine was supposed to be. The first person I ever told about the bed, how I dreamt of returning to it night after night and setting a lighter to the edge of its sheets, deemed me unfit to speak of it too. That my memory had served its purpose. That the damage was done, and I could have avoided it.

I carry every excuse anyone has ever made for him behind me like a knapsack of stars. It is not the good that burns brightly, but *he was drunk and he couldn't help himself with a body as beautiful as yours* that turn into a lantern I can't seem to let go of. The kind that lights the path ahead but only into the jaws of the lion.

In the news, a woman is found living with the three bodies of her dead children. They were there for years, rotting away quietly into the background while the neighbors went about their lives without ever knowing. This is how I live now too, the ways I was hurt tucked into the pockets of my ribcage, the crime scene of my body closed and unnoticeable to outside observers, all because I was born with an apology already clenched between my teeth.

THE POET THINKS OF WAYS TO UNDO THE SITUATION

What if I had spilled my guts instead of not having the guts
to let you have sex with me?
What if spilling my guts meant yelling louder?
The hunter draws back the bow with the arrow in his mouth
before shooting the deer. I should have listened
to the warning sound of it being let loose when you slid into me
or pulled its rough edges out of my skin and forgotten about it.
Shouldn't it be a relic by now?
Under the earth in the burial ground of my memory?
But this is what I do: I polish it every night until it glows,
keep it cupped in my palm,
heavy in my pocket, let others hold its weight.
I could have thrown it away.
Scientists say women are born with all the eggs they'll ever have
and there's no way to turn that into poetry.
Instead I spend my days tiptoeing over all their shells
covering my floorboards
as if landing with a softer step next time
would have pulled you away from my body
and out the window
you broke in through.

WHEN HE ASKED IF I WOULD WRITE ABOUT IT

The first time he forced my legs apart like marionette strings
in the hands of a misguided puppeteer,
He asked, "You gonna write about me?"
The second time, with his fingers making bruises on my neck,
he asked the same question.
So the third time, when I was beaten down
like a piano beyond repair,
all broken keys and a slowly dwindling melody,
I wrote about him.
I wrote, "I beatbox with ghosts. I got a handful of knives in my back
from all the times people like you stabbed me
when I was just starting to turn around."
I wrote, "Land of the free, home of the brave,
but you're just the coward
who didn't even bother to ask my name. I got a heartbeat
like a pendulum, it swings so fast
you'll never even know what hit you.
You'll never break my heart. It'll break you."
When he apologized over texts a few weeks later
then forced another woman the way he forced me,
I started slipping the poems under his front door,
beneath the windshield wiper
of his car, inside the sleeve of his pillowcase.
He asked me if I would write about him.
So I did.
I wrote about him to anybody who would listen,
until my final poem ended up in the hands of the police.
Then I pulled all the knives out of my back
and severed all the blame I'd aimed at myself for so long.

I keep having sex. I can't stop. Ride the subway trying not to think about killing myself, draw circles in the frosted windows while the other riders stare like who's this girl who can't keep her hands to herself. Wasn't that you who couldn't? Get up in the morning just to fry eggs because I gotta eat something to keep myself alive only to think about trauma until the butter crisps in the pan and all the eggs turn black. Like the current state of my life, am I right? I keep having sex. I can't stop. Men in my bed one after the other sometimes several in one night. Sometimes it hurts like a knife. Then I should have known better when he carved me up, shouldn't I? Should've seen it coming from a mile away. Go to work and cry in the office at the gorgeous fullness of the afternoon moon outside the window. In a world beautiful as this, why is violence such a common practice?

Use up all three of my free wine vouchers in a single evening. Can hardly wait until the doorbell rings the next day and they arrive in full, fifteen bottles of dark ruby, down them down them down them until I can't remember my own name. I keep having sex. I can't stop. Only do it while drunk, this is how I cope. Wishing like King Midas these men will turn me into gold.

But you turned me into ashes, shouldn't I know better? The first time you held my palms back against the bedposts, shouldn't I have left you?

Why didn't I see it? I could have saved myself, couldn't I have?

MAGICIAN AS HOSTAGE

The magician in me, if the long end of the wishbone is pulled,
will plant a daisy in the hole where my heart was uprooted
so instead of counting sheep each night before bed
my lungs will tear out its petals with the words *It was your fault,
it was your fault not* alternating with each pull.
   The trick in which the woman's body
   appears to be cut in half while the audience screams
   doesn't apply here.
   The rapist took care of that for me.
   If I, the magician, call him *my* rapist,
   does the spell wear off?
   Does the responsibility become mine
   instead of his?
Like a rabbit from a hat the truth comes out.
I kissed him first. With tongue. There was a little blood
when he bit my lip, and I enjoyed it.
I fought what came after but there was no switchblade
hidden beneath my pillow, no dove to abracadabra into a lion
whose teeth & claws would scare him out of my bed.
   The legend goes like this: if I wanted it at first,
   then I must have wanted it the whole time.
   I've been told that so many times
   that even my bones started to internalize it
   the way the audience always believes
   the magic is real.

WINTER

It's January and I'm watching men breakdance
in the middle of a snowy street
feeling full of moondust and firejazz,
hoping my pulse won't betray me.
If anyone was wondering, I still feel desire.
Summer was when it happened.
Summer I carry in my belly
but not the kind of summer
filled with tanning oil
or cool banks of pool water
the kind of summer filled with sweat
and fear on a queen bed
waiting waiting waiting
until the moment was over.
I still want these men on this street
and all their dance moves in the bedroom.
Still want them to kiss me so hard my spine cracks
want their mouths on my neck, nails on my back
want them to slide into me like syrup.
Does that mean I wanted summer too?
Does that mean I lit the fire that replaced my body with soot?
It's January and I'm watching men breakdance
in the middle of a snowy street
hoping my pulse won't betray me.

HOME INVASION

The night after, I dream about a room with three doors,
all unlocked. I can only enter one but can open all three.
The first door leads into a room with all windows.
The next with a circle of candles and a pillar of salt
frosting the floorboards.
The third with a single bed.
I enter the third and never come back out.
They all tell you it wasn't your fault,
there was nothing you could have done.
I could have entered the first room and left through the windows.
I could have entered the second and the Ouija board
would have told me what was about to happen.
But I entered the third and the entire house burned down.
They always tell you that you can put out the flames,
that it will happen, it's possible, it gets better.
But no one ever talks about where to find the water.

THE SAD CARTOGRAPHY OF LOSS

The crowd lays out the body inside the dark museum,
the night guards as witnesses, letting what needs to be done
be done. Here, the windpipe that chose not to scream,
the Achilles heel arched in steadfast beauty like a bridge,
toes curled as if ready for flight.
The paleontologist interrupts.
And yet she did not run when she had the chance
goes back to brushing the individual bones of the ribcage
that house the heart
that should have known.
Here, the kneecaps whose cartilage stretched and creaked
when standing up, that anchored the legs buried deep
in the ocean of bed, that should have swam away
when he turned his back
for one split second.
The hands with their piano fingers,
built from comet tails and solar flare
yet never harnessed the wind
to shove him away.
This is the body that lies open on the museum floor
being dusted for fingerprints
that the entire crowd believes, even the night guards,
she could have prevented.

ANGER

There are so many flavors of rage. The fuck-you-how-could-you-do-this-to-me kind, the why-did-this-happen-to-me-of-all-people kind, the please-god-let-this-just-be-a-dream kind. The rage that comes on so suddenly it makes you sob, makes you smash every single plate in the cupboard until the sound of breaking porcelain turns into muscle memory. This is the kind of anger that will break you. But this is the kind of anger that is justified.

"NOT ALL MEN"

My grandmother cracks eggs the same way the man
who invaded her house locked the bedroom door
and wouldn't let her leave until he was finished: fierce & loud,
with purpose, as if whatever came spilling
out of her body would be useful.
With eggs, there is only yolk. With my grandmother, there was life.
And I live in fear of dark alleyways and drinks filled with drugs
that lead to blackout and some stranger's fingers in my mouth
because inside my twenty years of life there was once a bed,
and another person in it,
and a moment that happened beneath the covers
in which my body was changed irreparably-
less a moment really, than a timeline I will never be rid of.
So you say not all men, not all men are werewolves
dressed like sheep who howl at the moon even when the moon
covers its ears and asks them to stop and they won't, they won't,
because stop is not a word they bothered to add
to their vocabulary; you say not all men, not all men, not all men.
But here we are, my grandmother and I, countless other women
who contain multitudes of bruises and memories
like wounds filled with salt
with skins that are afraid to occupy themselves
after already being occupied by so many trespassers.
And all you can do is stand there and say not all men,
but let this poem spit in your face
that we know, we know, we women are not stupid,
we know not all men do what so many have already done to us,
but this is the least helpful thing to say
because the wrong that some men do
makes us scared of all the others.
This is not balm for our stitches; this is tearing them open.
Say *too many men* instead.
And there
is some kind of progress.

THE POET DESTROYS HER APARTMENT IN A FIT OF RAGE

While reading a zine about these kinds of things, these assaults and bruises, I come across my story on a page halfway through. The narrator has every minute detail down pat, the way he fell asleep beside me afterward, the vanilla candle on the bedside table, the owl cooing outside the window that seemed like it was serenading me. This is when the panic sets in like molasses- I imagine every sparrow dies at once, a ring of wings plummeting to the ground, imagine a fault line opening up beneath my house to swallow all the apartments like birthday cakes with shards of glass stuck inside the batter for windows. I don't know how this narrator knows my story, I don't know who told them, did someone hire a private investigator to follow me? This is when the drinking starts. This is when a bottle of wine turns into two. This is when I start writing poems about my assault, slurring every inked line, yes drunk poets slur on paper too, and when I am finished I post the poem on my blog because at this point drunk is drunk is too drunk to care, and receive a message in my inbox like a lantern shining from a lighthouse and there it is, the other person somewhere halfway across the world thanking me for my poem. It is, they say, just like their own story.

This is when I realize. There was no private investigator. No one was watching through the windows as he put his hands on me and didn't stop.

Someone else simply went through the same hell I did. There are many different hells and we just happen to share the same one.

This is what I call anger. This is what I call too much. This is what I call an unnecessary coincidence. This is what I call reading a story in a zine that seems like my own story but it's the story of more people than I can count.

This is what I call me smashing all the wine goblets in my cupboard against the wall until I can finally see something that isn't red.

PYROMANIAC

My mama calls me the arsonist because in my mind
I've burned the dress I was wearing that night into cinders
more times than I can count.
Twenty thousand oceans in the world and not a single one
can put out the fire.
Mama, you don't know that some nights I set that cigarette lighter
to the edge of my pillow, vow to cut off all my hair,
make plans to dig a hole in the backyard for every reminder.
But mama, everything in my life reminds me of that evening;
the only way to forget is to turn the hole into a grave
and pull the dirt over my head like an eiderdown.
But you still kiss my forehead every morning,
tell me I'm the best daughter you could ever hope to have,
oblivious to this rage that spins my windpipe into a windstorm,
my bones into steel, every breath so hot in my chest
it feels like a volcano is being reincarnated from a forest fire.
Mama, mama, with all this anger I've got,
the next hurricane will be named after me,
and it will not leave his house untouched.

SOME KIND OF "FUCK YOU" EULOGY

Your apology means nothing. This has to stop happening. Stop hurting people, stop burying them inside their beds like graves, we are not skeletons, we are not ghosts, we deserve to live like everyone else. This isn't love, this isn't love, this isn't how you show women you love them, you show them with kind hands and a soft heart and grace and more sugar than salt. You thought all this meant nothing! You thought my body could be gutted like a fish with a switchblade and I would clean up the blood all by myself, that this is routine, that just because this has happened to me before, hooked on the end of a line while I'm drowning in plain air, means you could do it to me again and I would forgive you. This isn't forgiveness. This is me shouting even though this is not in all caps, it shouldn't have to be in all caps for you to know that this is wrong, what you did was wrong, this is anger and I hope you are listening, this isn't putting a seashell to your ear and hearing the ocean, this is putting a seashell to your ear and hearing a goddamn tsunami on the other end.

ANNIE OAKLEY

In which I continue living with the man who hurt me
because he constantly apologizes and I foolishly believe
in every "I'm sorry" :
> Someone has left the blood oranges in the freezer again.
> Last month I would remove them, inspect them for frostbite,
> place them back into the lower fridge drawer.
> Now I lie awake at night with his warm body next to me
> listening for pops from downstairs as their cold red innards
> explode into sweet pulp that I will have to scrape off
> in the morning.

This is not a warm body I feel safe with;
this is him holding a salt shaker to my wounds
when I ask for pepper instead.
> After the first time it happened he looked me in the eyes,
> gave me tissues to wipe my mouth and apologized
> for so long
> that the wall clock's screen almost burst
> like glasses do in the hands of opera singers.

But it doesn't stop happening
and this is a truth I wish I could cast a spell on
to turn into a lie.
> He vows daily to never touch me without permission again,
> brings home roses of every color,
> serves me breakfast in bed with French toast and bacon.
> Dinner is always made when I come home.
> And this is why I stay. The promises are so good
> I believe them.

But the cycle repeats itself like some sort of never-ending evolution
of cocoons into butterflies and butterflies back into cocoons.
At night, drunk or sober, he holds my legs apart
and whispers *I love you's* the whole time
like they can erase the damage.
> One night after this I gather the frozen fruit
> from the freezer,
> take the rifle from the garage
> and place each orange on a coffee can,
> shoot to my heart's desire.
> I empty the gun of bullets until they lie
> in a sunset mess on the grass
> like bloody valentines.

ASTRONAUT FAIRYTALE

Do not ask me the following:
What I was wearing.
How much I had to drink, if anything.
If I screamed.
If I struggled verbally or physically.
If it all started off consensually.
If I somehow enjoyed it.
Or if I came.

The only fact that matters is that this thing is a vampire. It bleeds me dry and leaves bite marks on my neck instead of hickeys. And no I don't have garlic, or a stake, or anything of the sort that will kill it. I can't escape it. Don't tell me I should "just get over it."

If I could get over it easily I would have climbed up the ladder and been halfway to the moon by now. I'd keep climbing, rung after rung, until the craters arrived to meet me, until I could look down from them on earth. A sad view to be sure, but at least then I'd be over it. Above it.

But that's fantasy. This is reality. Keep the two straight.

RUMPELSTILTSKIN

When the miller's daughter couldn't spin the straw into gold,
Rumpelstiltskin promised to do so for her
if she gave her firstborn child to him in return.
When I confided in my poetry professor months later
he told me to spin my anger into something beautiful
and this is what no one seems to understand:
      Nothing about this can be turned into gold.
      Nothing about this is poetic even as I write about it now.
      A poet is in no way King Midas;
      the only thing I can spin this into is blood.
At night before sleep I pray to the man in the moon instead
because the only God I know
would not let this happen to me
and keep happening.
The man in the moon never answers;
I guess that's what they call a long-distance relationship.
      Yes I would give my firstborn child away
      if it meant turning this into something beautiful.
      No I would not think twice
      and if this makes me a bad person
      then I am willing to be the worst one on earth.

TO MY SONS WHEN THEY ASK ABOUT OYSTERS AND PEARLS

To my sons I will tell the tale of the woman
who swallowed the pearl while eating oysters soaked in gin.
Teach them to hide switchblades beneath their pillows
for fighting off intruders only.
Wear their gentleness like grace.
This is not the kind of world I would have wanted to grow up in.
But I did, I did, more growing pains than growing gains.
Will teach them *no* does not mean *change my mind,* does not mean
keep kissing me until I give up, does not mean
touch me here and here and here
does not mean *fuck me over or fuck me fuck me fuck me*
it means *no and fuck you if you think otherwise.*
Will tell them of the women who sleep in whale carcasses
washed up on the beach for weeks on end
because they're too afraid to go home to their husbands.
Will tell them Eve did not belong to Adam
even though she evolved from his rib, tell them tell them tell them
the birds and the bees should exclude the bees
because sex shouldn't sting.
Please, I will tell them, treat your partner like honey.
They will ask me what became of the woman
who swallowed the pearl–
Where did the pearl go? Isn't it worth something? Can we take it?
And then I will tell them, no, you take what is yours
and nothing more.

THE CURE FOR LONELINESS

The Ancient Greeks placed coins over the eyes of the dead
in order to pay the ferryman to row them across the river
and into the afterlife.
Yesterday I collected all the loose change from inside the pockets
of the sweater I was wearing that night
and buried them in my backyard next to 54 empty beer bottles
and a jar of rain.
The next person who unearths these fossils won't be me
because they're already on their way to the next life.
Let me yell from the rooftops what everyone already knows:
I am getting there. I am making it.
My neurons are learning how to reshape themselves
into something that isn't about you anymore.
One day I'll go back to the tree we once carved our initials in
and teach the roots to let go too.
The other night I listened to a looped recording
of my own whisper
on repeat and turned up the volume
until it drowned out the thunderstorm
banging the shutters against the house.
It would be a mistake to say windowpanes know nothing of pain.
It would be a mistake to say I'm going to allow you to force me to
keep whispering.
I've already paid more than my fair share to cross over
from what you did to me.
This is my afterlife now. Not yours.
Let's keep it that way.

PERSEPHONE

Persephone rules the underworld with the grace of spring
and the bravery of winter.
But dressing the souls of the dead with the curses of men
wasn't enough to prevent Hades from carrying her off
like the sea spins a ship into a shipwreck.
These nights, the left hemisphere of my brain is just a piano
with all the strings cut out
so it won't have to play the music of your memory anymore.
The right hemisphere still wants to fuck you
not in the sense of rocking the bed,
but in the sense of fucking you over
so you get a taste of your own medicine.
Sometimes Persephone wishes to bake the sheaf of grain
she began carrying after Hades abducted her
into a loaf of bread to get a taste of her own sadness too.
But Persephone, Persephone, she was not to blame
it is not hers to consume
and even though all this comes with an ocean of shame
I refuse to crash against the rocks you laid out for me
when I was already having difficulty
keeping my head above water.
Maybe one day I'll rule over your hell
just like Persephone.

SEARCHING FOR SOLACE

Searching for solace in the midst of trauma, sometimes in dangerous ways. Anything to feel even a little bit better. Sometimes through drinking, sometimes thinking, sex, smoking, running, music. Wanting to piece the light bulb back together and find its light again. You do what you do in order to survive. You cope how you can.

SAD OMELETS

Superstition warns that breaking open an egg
and finding two yolks inside
means someone you know will either get married or have twins.
I imagine my mother, the four of us crowding the amniotic fluid
inside her womb like mermaids whose tails were only nubs
and had not get begun to grow glistening with scales,
how her joy sprouted a backbone of grief
when the doctor informed her the smallest child was dead.
      In a city of hands, mine would be the first
      to shy away from all the others,
      to read their palm lines and callouses from a distance
      to determine whether they'd ever bloodied themselves
      inside someone else's body
      and thus if I should stay away from their owners.
The worst nightmares involve the entire landing of the house
covered in double-yolked eggshells to tiptoe over
this fear that stepping on one and crushing it underfoot
would kill the twin versions of myself that never had to fight
to survive beneath someone else's body in the soft hollow of a bed.
      Strange, how all this grief that houses itself inside my spine
      carries the exact weight of the sibling
      my mother never had.

BOYFRIEND COURT

My brain is only an alibi for all the damage my heart causes. My mother's body is only a mold I was poured into before my insides cooled. This is how I have learned to love: in metaphors, in figurative language that bites its tongue to avoid saying the things worth saying, even if it means drawing blood. This is what I learned love is: a chorus of axes serenading the pear tree inside my heart that grew from a single seedling. Most lovers I've had don't bother to count the number of rings lodged inside its base before fucking me. They're more concerned with it bearing fruit.

This is what I do: feed the mouth of loneliness by playing a drinking game whenever memories of the night I learned I was too small for my body to be handled gently return to me. Drink every time his voice lurches back into my head, every time I come across his name in headlines, internet posts, whispered by my grandmother to my mother when they think I can't hear. Swallow for every time I flinch at touch. Sink my head into the toilet bowl like a first kiss with tongue for every time the cocktails make me vomit.

This is how I love now: heart clenched like a fist. There is no other option but this. All men who ask to sleep with me are guilty until proven innocent. The trial that determines the verdict? Their eyes must look nothing like his. They can't wear his favorite brand of cologne, have to undress me as if readying for a feast instead of an autopsy. Their first, middle, and last names must bear no resemblance to his own. They cannot be his blood relatives, cannot have ever met before, strangers since birth.

The most important factor: they must not be him.

GRETEL GETS DRUNK

(In another life, there was no Hansel.
There was only Gretel, and instead of a witch eating her alive,
it was an apartment, and a small mattress,
and a man who looked harmless
before he locked the bedroom door.
Thankfully Gretel had left a trail of breadcrumbs behind her
across the sidewalks & into the streets
that she used as a map for returning home.)

And this is how Gretel lives now:

> She wakes early to crack eggs for omelets and somehow
> can never manage not to cry into the french toast
> batter. This is why she never has any breakfast guests. She
> doesn't want the ones she loves ingesting her tears. There
> are good days and bad days; there are pills and then there
> are poems. Gretel gets drunk an average of twice a day. This
> means she lives in a constant state of hangover and
> recovering-from-previous-hangover and any contact
> with men involves gin and whiskey and sometimes a
> combination of white wine and screwdrivers. This is not
> the best way to live. To be afraid of sex but to use it as a
> means of survival. To be drunk so often that drunk becomes
> the new sober.

> This is how Gretel lives now, and it's been months since she
> baked bread, or added croutons to her salad, because these
> are the maps she once followed to escape, and no reminders
> of that night are good.

BLUEPRINTS FOR TATTOOS THAT MAKE THE OWNER WEEP

Last night I discovered a birthmark on the back of my neck
in the shape of someone leaving.
Joy always abandons me like all the other men in my life do—
sweet release through the front door and back,
vaulting over the railings,
even out the emergency exit at the side of the bar.
Men hang around my tailbone like chandeliers; they stay there
until my lights go out.
The trouble is, I'm almost always dark.
The worst and best pickup line I've ever heard
went deep like an eye socket:

"Being with you never requires any effort
because you're so engulfed in sadness
that anything at all will appeal to you."

The difference between almost and lost
is just two extra letters.
The difference between sadness and joy
is so many letters that the entire alphabet
forgets its purpose.

ANOTHER ONE OF THOSE MATRYOSHKA POEMS

1.   I opened a photograph of my mother and inside the
     photograph I found all the love letters from my father
     that were singed in the house fire when my brother
     left a cigarette stubbed into the carpet.

2.   I opened the love letters and found crisp brown edges.

3.   I opened the edges and found.

Fast forward. None of this matters except for the autopsy.
When they gently peel back my ribcage they'll find some
bullshit heart that continues beating for no reason
in particular, like a pigeon
that carries all the wrong messages.
They'll find twenty bottles of wine and fifteen
used condoms from all the sex I used to feel better
instead of the hospital,
three ticket stubs for airplane trips to islands
with exotic names
(I used all my frequent flyer miles as a way of escaping),
bedtime stories from my grandmother, a collection of
quotes from friends and loved ones all involving
the words *you don't deserve this pain*
and a beehive of sleeping pills
except with this, there is no honey to pour in the wound
only salt.

ON HAVING SEX WITH STRANGERS JUST TO FEEL OKAY

When I was young, my grandmother taught me the shortest distance
between two people is the distance they are willing to walk
to reach one another.
At night I light cigarettes like signal flares one after the other until
every new man whose bed I show up to
thinks I'm carrying this fire for him.
This is the way my body loves: it only understands itself
when connected to someone else's,
the way people who drown in vats of grain
only realize when the air stops coming in
that sometimes the worst that can happen to us
is actually quite beautiful.
That I can have my mother's teeth
and my father's chin, my sister's laugh
and my grandmother's palms, but I would trade them all in
for a chance to live inside someone else's skin.
Every night before I fall asleep within the arms of a man
who thinks it was love
when it was really just sex, I wonder for the briefest of seconds
if the shortest distance I would walk
would be to myself.

SOMETIMES MY BODY IS ACCEPTABLE

To some people, sleeping alone
means sleeping without another person by their side.
To me, sleeping alone would mean sleeping
in an entirely different body
than the one I was hurt in.
Tonight, I am making cocktails out of ghosts, hoping someone
from the bar next door will be willing to look past my scar tissue
and discover the orchestra beneath it, someone
who will crescendo the skipped beats in my pulse
into a symphony in which the conductor finally forgets
about wanting to be dead.
Tonight, I remember my grandparents
shelling crabs beneath the stars
her head tucked into the crook of his neck,
the way their bodies formed the shape of acceptance.
Tonight, I invite a litany of men into my bed in the hopes that,
for just a few split seconds, my body will form the same shape.
For the person on the other side of the mirror
to be the person my mother always wanted her to be.
To finally look at my bones
and see not a cage
but a museum.

SEX & BINGE-DRINKING

I can't have sex sober anymore. I'm always drinking when I'm sinking into someone else's body. This is what I carry like a match within me; this is the only thing I still have left that no one will blow out. Inside my bedroom it's not a monster beneath the bed. It's you. Maybe because you used my skin as a house I now use it as my canvas to tear down. Let me make mixed drinks out of lovers, out of all the men I've ever slept with. Some like it rough. They push my hands back against the bed until all my bones creak like a haunted house. Maybe this is what I am. Scaring everyone else away until no one wants to come in. On the upper floor of my heart someone is screaming out a window but no one on the street will listen. She just keeps going and going and won't stop. It was a mistake to think anyone would have time to pay attention to something that sad.

JUST ANOTHER LOVE POEM. UNTIL THE FIRST LINE.

No one ever teaches you how to fall out of love with your rapist.
How to survive until the moment when their shadow ceases to be
an extension of your own, how to find someone else
to be your North Star
who won't ever violate the rest of your sky.
How to recognize wolves in sheep's clothing,
or wolves that devour you
then bring you the remains of a dead dove as a peace offering
like its feathers are enough to erase the teeth marks.
No one ever teaches you how to stop looking into a bedroom
and seeing the person you love sitting next to the window, waiting,
seeing your rapist sitting there too
and realizing they are one and the same.
No one ever teaches you that it could take years
before you stop feeling like a crescent moon and more like a full one,
that it takes eons to cut the strings connecting you
to the person who said I love you and it's your fault
in the same tone of voice
when all you want is to hand them the scissors
and keep the strings intact.
And most of all, no one talks about wishing to feel their skin
on yours again
even after months of being torn in half.

MAMMOTH

Listen, there are lambs and there are lions
and then there are crosses between the two, some hybrid of pulse
and snarl, some witches' brew of softness and teeth.
Paleontology calls them mammoths;
I call them the first man and the second man,
the fifth and the last. They pinned me to walls with their tusks
branded me as their own like a butterfly mounted on a corkboard.
The wooly body was just a disguise- this is no tale of a wolf
raising a human child as its own
and protecting it from the rest of the pack;
this is what I took to be safety
but was taught I should have known better.
My sister claims to have seen one once, its giant loping body
crossing the shadow of my room at night
the door closing before it found me huddled beneath the sheets.
Unlike a vampire, garlic and stakes won't keep it away
the spoiled eggs I line my windows with to ruin its appetite for me
only serve to entice it further.
Paleontologists have pronounced mammoths extinct
but for me, they could never be more alive.

HEALING

Healing: the slow evaporation of bruises, on skin, heart, and mind. The moments when you allow love to hold you and to trust in it again, when your body stops feeling like a bomb shelter or a graveyard without flowers on any of its headstones, and starts feeling like a home again. These are manifestos to survival and overcoming.

BEAUTY & THE BEAST

When the daughter came to her mother with stained underwear
and cramps so fierce they rivaled the bravery of a thousand wolves,
mother told daughter to drink cranberry juice
until it eased the stitches in her side.
When men slid their hands into and around daughter's body,
cupped her breasts without warning and kissed the soles of her feet,
daughter mixed the cranberry juice with vodka instead
but soon enough mother came to the rescue,
mother who was born with all the eggs she'd ever keep,
mother with her hands shaping dough
into warm loaves in the kitchen,
mother with a spine built from crawl spaces filled with secrets.
She taught daughter how to fall in love with shadows
that would protect her,
how to make ghosts out of fear in order to exorcise them,
how to use poetry as balm and salve,
how sometimes the beast is disguised as the beauty.
To find the deep end of healing
and launch herself into it.

REMINDER FROM MY HEART TO MY HEAD

Love, and love, and love, and let this be your alibi when the cops come knocking, asking where you buried your own body and if you can lead them to the gravesite. Let love be what you were doing when you disappeared without a trace. When birds slam belly-up into your windows remind yourself it was not your fault they saw a life they wanted into but miscalculated the distance.

Let there be more than birthdays, let there be anniversaries for every month you survived. Let there be a lopsided cake weighed down by candles for celebrating the birth of the sparrow inside your throat that you fed with birdseed night after night in the dark until it grew plump and soft and siphoned your voice up through your windpipe and into the open air again. Don't be afraid to get sugar stuck in the creases of your palms, flour smeared across the nape of your neck, to spread the batter across the floor and make snow angels in its sticky sweetness like a chalk outline at a crime scene. Remember, though, you are no longer a crime scene and have lived to tell the tale.

Love as a form of quiet revenge. Lick the plate of survival clean and leave your belly hungry for more. It will never betray you. This thing will no longer hang upside down over your head like a bat in the rafters. This will no longer undo you. There's no need to buy an entire castle full of deadbolts for your body anymore, to be afraid of the man who could pick the locks.

You have survived, and will continue to do so.

THE SECRET HEALING POWERS OF LOBSTERS

A friend tells me lobsters are immortal.
In biology language this means
their rate of mortality either decreases
or remains stable across the lifespan.
For dinner my mother serves them with
steaming red shells still attached,
wrapped in butter with herbs whose names
I know as well as my own skin.
Family legend tells of the time my great-great-grandmother
accidentally cooked her wedding ring into the lobster salad
only discovering the mistake when her husband
bit down hard on the tarnished silver;
in this way love is immortal too.

> But I started out loving incorrectly
> thinking all that mattered about the first man
> I ever slept with
> was that his heart murmured
> when I laid my ear to it
> not how he handled my body
> like its existence was insignificant.

I know better now,
can love in fistfuls instead of fingertips,
map out my new partner's body entirely by heart
the same way a person searching for the bathroom
in the middle of the night
has to cling to the walls to find their way.

> And our family still cooks lobsters for reunion dinners
> my parents holding hands beneath the table
> my great-great-grandparents long dead & gone
> but the love they shared lives on.

AMEN, AMEN, AMEN

For one week at college I sleep with three different men,
yes this is a true story, and no, not once do I have a panic attack.
The usual ritual before sex is this: get drunk
because it eases the fear, makes it docile
like sedating a lioness,
practice the position that will be easiest to escape from.
Remind myself my lungs are airplanes
and beneath each rib is another love letter
from my heart to my head.
But this time I drink the champagne from thimbles
instead of shot glasses,
can kiss each man with my eyes closed,
feel my way across his body blind
without having to watch his hands like a hawk
to make sure they are situated
where they are supposed to be.
This week I let them stay in my bed after the sex is finished,
this week I am not afraid to let them stay
and when we are wound round each other like muscle memories
there is another language inside my mouth
besides the many others I already carry,
the language of safety without fear.

RESUMING DATING 101 FOR SURVIVORS

Someone asks me on a date.
Someone asks me on a date and the familiar tornado rises
in my stomach;
instead of butterflies when I get nervous
now there are natural disasters.
The date begins with bedroom and ends up with dinner-
sometimes reverse psychology allows the birds egg
to travel back up into the nest
before it explodes on the pavement,
and this is why I view the date backwards:

1. He undressed me like taking a cicada out of its shell, handled
   the small bone nubs on my shoulders with grace where
   the first man tore out my wings as if uprooting an onion.

2. Before everything, he asked. Even before kissing. My tongue
   was only ever inside his mouth when it wanted to be.

3. There was something buried inside the dusk of my skin
   that felt like desire again. Something unfamiliar for months-
   déjà vu for the overly-nostalgic.

4. When he slid inside me, it was good. It was slow.
   There was never a moment when I panicked.

5. Somewhere inside me there were fireworks.
   Somewhere on his face there was something like love.
   Yes I survived. But there was nothing to survive
   because all of it was beautiful,
   all of it was mutual,
   none of it hurt.

Afterward our bodies fly back to the restaurant
and the waiter gets both orders correct on the first try
and the whole time he cares about what I have to say
and I am thinking that maybe, just maybe,
I will feel safe sleeping with him later.
And I do.

THE EVOLUTION OF EVE

Adam rises from dust and Eve rises from his ribs.
And for a while Adam tastes the salt inside Eve's bones
and spins it into sugar, and Eve truly believes
the way she comes apart in his hands
is a good thing.
But the months go by and Eve's blood sings like a bird
on its way to crossing the equator
with something still tethering it to the earth,
and Eve, Eve is tired of being treated as a papier-mâché body
that Adam handles with palms like matches,
and how she must give herself to him
anytime he asks.
At night when he is asleep, his arms threaded around her shoulders
like a black widow's spiderweb, she reads tales of King Midas
and how everything he touched turned to gold,
so Eve closes her eyes and wishes, hard as she can,
until the trees turn to gold leaf and the rivers run molten yellow
and she touches the forbidden fruit from the tree
until it solidifies into gold.
Then Eve herself becomes a statue worth millions
who will never move nor speak again,
and Adam, Adam will never be able to have her
anytime he wants anymore,
nor eat the forbidden fruit from the tree that would have him exiled,
and so it is that Adam learns that women must not be caged
and must live alone in Paradise for the rest of his days
with no way to eat the fruit and escape.
And so it is that Adam learns how sometimes,
what Paradise is for one
is hell for another.

THE LITTLE MERMAID LEARNS TO KEEP HER HEAD ABOVE WATER

Once, I dyed my hair to change colors with the seasons
and finally settled on red out of the mistaken belief
that it would lend me all the courage fire lends to wood.
Beneath the wave caps a merman once did something to me
that made me wish to slice open my lifelines
on the sharp edges of a coral reef.
Now, I remember my legs, my phantom limb syndrome,
how I used to run so fast along the shore
even the seagulls couldn't catch me.
Those were the days when my head was still above water,
when I never once thought of shedding the scales on my wrists
and ending it all.
One day I'll go back to those legs, to coming up out of the deep
and tasting the salty air again
without wishing to drown.
One day seaweed will stop reminding me of a noose.
One day I will trust again with lungs full of fresh air.
There are still so many seashells on the shore left to collect,
and I'm finally going to find them all.

THE SURVIVOR'S MANIFESTO

Let me be perfectly clear and by clear I mean I am clearing this out of the way now so it will never be more rubble to clean up in the future, and by clearing this out of the way I mean clearing it out of my way and putting it into yours. I want this to be your roadblock, your dead end, the deer you have to swerve to avoid late at night in the dark.

I am reclaiming the language I spoke on the night I said no and you did not listen. It was not a foreign language. It was a language everyone knows, a language that from the moment of birth builds a home between our bones and assumes that it will be heard and not ignored, that no one will ever set fire to its door and pick the deadbolt.

But this is not a language that you cared enough to speak back. That language was respect and you spoke back with disrespect, and by disrespect I mean you waited until my No died from so many times of repeating it and then reincarnated it into what you would later call a yes. But what you forgot is that I didn't forget. I searched for that no far and wide where you had hidden it and I found it and said, This is the wrong skin you are wearing. You are wearing the skin he gave you and it's full of bruises. Come back to me. You and I know who you really are.

So tonight I am taking my No back and erasing its bruises. I am taking back the black eye you gave it when it refused to look you in the eye.

Listen, the rain falls hard some days. I hope you fall hard too. I hope the rest of your days are filled with potholes and storms that never end. And do not think that I will feel sorry for you. Apologies are not reserved for something that someone deserved, and you deserve hurricanes. You deserve monsoons and you deserve standing on the roof of your falling-apart life while everything else you hold near and dear washes away in the flood of what you could call the-rest-of-your-life. You deserve having nothing left to hold onto, not even driftwood.

Today I apologize to myself since you will not. I apologize for the way you made my body into a splintered sinking ship and then sailed away without a care in the world like most people do when someone else is drowning.

I apologize to myself for all the months in which no one believed me. I apologize to myself for the fact that when I spoke the truth, you called it a lie and as usual everyone believes the liar. I apologize to myself for the fact that I did not leave when I had the chance.

But I do not apologize to myself for giving myself another chance. For the nights I walked to bridges and stood on their railings and returned to solid ground at the last second. For the nights I held handfuls of pills like tickets into some better kind of afterlife and decided to wait for concert tickets instead.

I hope the rest of my life is the best of my life. Because I survived even when survival itself was having a hard time figuring out how to live up to its name.

Today I move on-ward. For-ward. Out-ward. I will grow.

Today, what are you?

Co-ward.

NATURAL DISASTER

In Turkmenistan a natural gas field opens itself
like a flaming envelope,
where it's been burning since 1971
referred to by locals as the Door to Hell.
It is enough to grow my hair out until its roots
burrow into the equator
until the ocean tugs it home like every strand is an anchor
keeping a line of ships in bottles tethered to earth.
It is enough to collect forks and knives in a shoebox beneath the bed
to use either as potential weapons or reminders of sorrow
and to not know yet which option to choose.
It is enough to save the spoons and string them up like windchimes
and to feel love at the sight of my reflection inside their silver curves
instead of a familiar disgust.
The Door to Hell burns and burns and burns
and has been for decades. Geologists don't know
when it will close over,
when the hole of it will heal and vanish into the ground
and it is enough to live with the wound, its constant ashes,
to sometimes feel an ache to step into it
and let the flames close over my head
but it is also enough
to have this wound exist in my life like a second sibling
and learn to get along with it.

THE PSYCHOLOGY OF THE MYTHOLOGY OF THE NEUROSCIENCE OF RECOVERY

This is what evolutionary psychologists will never teach you about Darwin: the two hemispheres of the human brain used to be one, until the gods held counsel and determined this allowed mere mortals too much feeling for a single body. So Zeus struck a thunderbolt into the soft skin of earth. This is how the brain separated itself into two halves. This is how the corpus callosum evolved to bridge them both.

Today, I use my right hemisphere like a shadowbox for all the bad memories, each one tucked into its own cupboard, the left hemisphere for all the good. Neuroscientists have proved the left hemisphere contains the brain's language center, its linguistic capabilities like no other. This is why I choose the left hemisphere for the good- so when I speak, only the beautiful comes out.

This is a way of reminding myself I am full of lightning like Zeus. That I am still whole despite the fact that my brain sleeps in two solitary beds like a divorced couple that can't reconcile even for the sake of their own children. And this is what evolutionary psychologists will never teach you about Darwin: evolution is not just a theory, but some kind of healing.

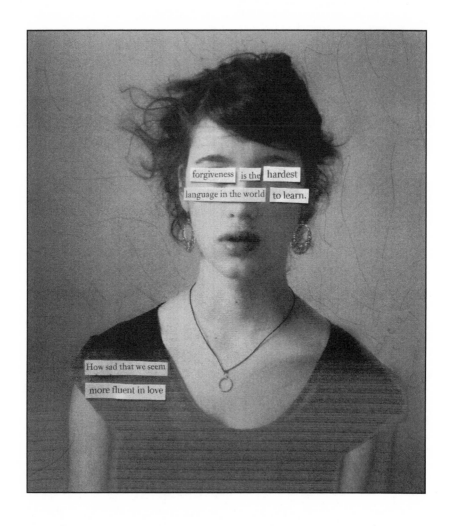

forgiveness is the hardest language in the world to learn.

How sad that we seem more fluent in love

FORGIVENESS

Letting go of the anger, the plans for revenge. Choosing not to. Making peace with your attacker. Wishing they'd go to hell. Moving on with your life and not hating them for the fact that you have to move on from something in the first place. Moving on with your life and still hating them. Forgiving or deciding not to. Whatever the choice is, as long as it's yours, it's the right one.

LESSONS MY MOTHER TAUGHT ME ABOUT LETTING GO

Don't live life with glass bones and tissue paper skin;
I birthed you to be stronger than that,
I built you from the universe instead.
I once had a messenger bird heart—
it didn't know which signal to send
so it sent all the wrong ones.
If you ever meet a man with a heart like that,
don't feed his heart with seeds
or let it perch on the windowsill of your soul.
Shoo it away, let it find somewhere else to land.
In waltzes one dance partner always carries a rose
between their teeth,
daughter, always carry mountain laurel instead;
every single part of it is deadly.
You were not raised to be beautiful,
you were raised to be brave.
There is forgiveness and then there is forgetting.
They are as different as salt and sugar,
but neither of them tastes sweet;
swallow one or swallow both, but never let anyone
tell you which to choose.
Joan of Arc burned for what she believed in,
and if you must do the same, then so be it.
But always remember to rise from the ashes like a phoenix.
Follow the seasons as a guide.
They will teach you how to accept change.

SOME THOUGHTS ON AMNESTY

When our biology teacher taught my middle school class
of how the female praying mantis
devours the male after mating,
that was the most important lesson
about forgiveness I have ever learned.
To go into love knowing it will tear you apart
yet embracing it with open arms
and giving it everything you have.

THE FORGIVENESS ANTHEM

Yesterday I did what most people do in spring: I did my fall cleaning. Swept out the brittle brown leaves from my body and opened up my skin to let the colorful ones in, let loose the moths from the closet where they'd been kept since last winter, breathing in dust.

Yesterday I stood beneath a full moon and listened as an owl cooed that single lonely question, "Who?" Me. This is me. My body, my pulse beneath these wrists, my freckles and bruises and bones and lines. Mine. My body is my shadowbox, the place I store everything beautiful and damaging, whether it will end up ruining me or not.

Once, a man cupped his hands around the soft outline of my hips and touched me like a comma before kissing me like an exclamation point.

Today, I am no question mark. I said no. I said no. There was no other punctuation following those two letters except a period. My bones. My body. My skin.

Once, my grandmother held both of my hands in her own and taught me to always leave stones behind. The day you split me open, I left pieces of gravel in the path you took out the front door after both of us had redressed and the morning light was growing dark pink. For every footstep, a pebble. All the way to your car where I later carved my initials into each side window.

I was here. So was my body. So were these stones.

Some nights I wake up sweating, hoping you swallow all those stones in your sleep until they form a mountain inside your stomach and shift around inside like a landslide, day after day until you know how it feels to carry around this weight. This weight that was not supposed to be mine but is now something like a second skin.

Once, a man brought with him a collection of hummingbirds and taught me the feather patterns that make each one unique, before releasing one into the sky and touching the small of my back.

Once, you did something that caged me, that pinned my feathers down and mounted me to your corkboard.

No longer.

I forgive you. I forgive you. I. Forgive. You.

Despite of all this and because of it, I forgive you.

NEW YEARS 2015

Girl was all I was ever taught to be. Girl with a body
poured into a mold the shape of something a man would love.
Girl swallowing molasses for breakfast so every word
in her windpipe would solidify like insects into amber
when no one would let her speak.
New Years Day 2015 and I have racked up
too many missed connections
with the moon: but at least the solar system can't follow me home
after too much to drink. Every heart carries different blood;
a transfusion requires some understanding that ghosts
mark & tag us like graffiti.
This is your art, this is my art, till death do us part.
The peeling back of the calendar page into an entirely new year-
like an onion, there may be some tears.
All that bullshit about the slate being wiped clean now,
the past being in the past
but I am still the girl who was only ever taught to be a girl.
Girl with a spine made of honey that every boy I slept with
sucked dry until I could not get away.
There was a heart somewhere inside me this year.
At one point it was a trapeze, another point
it was a summer filled with sparklers
that was not this year's summer because this year's summer
was what some people call rock bottom.
To conclude, if I could peer into the Rorshach inkblot of this year
and see a new & better year inside it,
this would be like winning the lottery.
To see some sort of pity for the men who hurt me,
to reach into my throat and find the dove of peace,
or an olive branch,
and offer it to them with open arms.

INSTRUCTIONS FOR DISCOVERING IF FORGIVENESS IS RIGHT FOR YOU

1.   There are no universal instructions. There is no universal handbook or blueprints to follow that will help you decide. Believe me, I've tried. I've held the bones of pain in my palms and tried to fit them back together into a skeleton that at least mildly resembles healing.

2.   Sometimes the skeleton collapses. Sometimes it gets up and waltzes for a while, tricks you into thinking it's strong enough to keep time, and then it breaks.

3.   Kissing another man who doesn't end up hurting you isn't forgiveness. It's called a man treating you right, the way you were supposed to be treated the first time around.

4.   There will be weeks when you want to take out your old baby teeth from the glass jar you've hid them in for years and go through each one individually, the incisors, the molars, to remind yourself that even things buried deep at the roots eventually learn to let go. Maybe that's forgiveness. Then again, maybe that's science.

5.   What's a grenade? It's a heart waiting to be thrown at the person who made it bleed. But keep it. Keep your heart. You've already lost enough. There are other ways to take revenge.

6.   Is revenge forgiveness? That's for you to decide. But I tend to think revenge means you're not over it yet.

7.   Love well, live well, and everything in between. You do that by cutting the strings they tied you down with. You let the strings go. You sleep in. You don't allow yourself to be tethered to that person anymore.

8.   What if that person was your lover? You learn how to love without them. It seems like the hardest thing in the world. Like retrieving stars from a black hole. But you do it you do it you do it you just have to. It will happen.

9. And when the time comes maybe you can tell them in person, or tell it to the world, or a piece of paper, or that secret place inside your mind, *I know what you did to me, but it didn't ruin me, I accept it without respecting it, and I have come to terms with it. And I don't hate you or myself; I hate what you did to me and why you thought it was okay.*

10. But that's your choice. That's your choice.

EMILY DICKINSON

In 1862 Emily Dickinson wrote 366 poems in 365 days
& over a century later the artist Spencer Finch
created an installation of 366 color-coded candles
to symbolize that year
then lit one each day until 12 months later
the ground was a melted sunset of wax.
> A poem is a poem is a poet is a person, you used to say.
> Everything I have is buried in salt.
> It used to be currency back in ancient times; this is how
> I remind myself Rome burned for six days & seven nights
> that Spencer's candles burned for an entire year,
> that somewhere inside me something is still burning too.
> A fire escape. An oil lamp. The poem
> you begged me not to write. About you. About this.
> About the way you snapped my spine like a wishbone
> & built it into an axe handle
> for cutting me down.

If Emily Dickinson's ghost visited me in a dream, or in this house,
or at my doorstep, I would follow in her footsteps.
Write down one good thing about you every day for a year,
hide each slip of paper in a glass bottle
& send them out to sea like 366 bobbing anchors
when all was said and done.
To remind myself that there was still good in you
despite the pain you put me through.
> But this is for people who believe in ghosts
> people for whom pity for their attackers arrives
> like a stray dog on their welcome mat
> & lies down panting at their feet.
> For people who let the dog stay.
> Who feed it until the ribs disappear.

THE LAST POEM I WRITE WON'T BE ABOUT YOU

Come here. I want to give you back all the stones
you slipped beneath my tongue to silence me,
to fill your hands with them until you finally realize
the years of weight you buried me under.
I want the sky back whole again, the exact same shade it was
when the storm that was you came into my life
carrying with it every tree it ever uprooted.
An old wives' tale from Russia spins a story
of how women in pain hung bird feathers from their clotheslines
until they finally felt light enough
to flee from the source of their hurt like sparrows.
The only difference between those feathers and me
is the feathers don't make a sound.
Come here- I want to give you my voicebox and my vocal cords,
every line on the back of my palms, the months of salt,
the way you used my body as kindling
to start your own fire.
Come here.
I want to give you my forgiveness for all the years you spent
putting my life on the line
just like those old Russian wives.

LOST APPETITE

On the worst days I knead my sorrow like bread,
let it rise and expand until it fills everything I am familiar with.
It feeds me well, makes a rich meal.
But there is something missing, in the way that bread without yeast
is not bread at all.
Something that feels like forgiveness, or at least the desire to forgive,
pushing against my ribcage.
I do not know what to do with this strange ingredient.
It wants to break my bones
so it can re-mend them.
How do I make room for this in my life
when so much has already been given to me that I did not want?
But it seems trustworthy, like a cat sleeping in one's lap
and trust is something I have been lacking.
So I let it stay.
Not for the year, but at least for the time being,
to see if it won't hurt me like all the others.

SOME THINGS YOU NEED TO KNOW IN ORDER TO FORGIVE YOURSELF

1. Most pain is only temporary, but other kinds of pain rise and spread like yeast into something too dense for any stomach to handle. The seeds of pain are the seeds we sow with our own hands— when we view our bodies as mistakes or as places to carve map lines into without having a clue about the destination.

2. Hands are the only parts of the body that speak real language. Whether they shake or remain still, whether they reach out or stay clenched, they reveal the entire universe.

3. Some parents tell their children they're beautiful because in the midst of a darkness that deep, they don't know what else to say. It doesn't mean their children aren't really beautiful; it just means that sometimes words aren't enough to close wounds.

4. When a couple throws salt over their shoulder at a wedding, it doesn't always symbolize a tradition or the start of a new life. In some cases, it just symbolizes a life being thrown away, a life both of them would rather have spent alone. Because sooner or later, we all end up wishing for silence.

5. It's not anarchy to love yourself. It's forgiveness.

6. Most of the time when someone lies awake at night and thinks about someone else so much that they're unable to fall asleep, it's because they'd rather be awake with the thought of another person besides themselves circling their head.

7. Some people love until the very end. The ones who love from the very beginning are the rarest of all.

8. That magic trick that involves an audience member's body supposedly being cut in half is really just a metaphor for breakups. One half of your body is your own, and the other half belongs to the person you used to be with. The hardest part is learning how to get rid of their half and become yourself again.

9. Tattoos represent all the words a person never had the courage to say aloud. Skin speaks louder than vocal cords ever could.

10. Regret is more powerful than any poison.

11. Sometimes home isn't a place, but a person.

12. Every neuron in the brain means something. Even though human beings are so complex, it's still too simple to be sad.

13. The greatest love affair you'll ever miss out on is yourself.

THE HISTORY OF GLACIERS

I want strange men to stop tracking me like bloodhounds,
to end this pull of their bodies to mine like the tides.
The best part of the dream is this: in a crowded room
everyone cheers for me to split the piñata with my fists
so they can feast on its insides
but at the last second, before I jolt awake,
it evolves into a wasp's nest.
I still find their brittle yellow bodies between the sheets
the wings long ago torn into confetti.
To be stung again and again and again, I don't want that anymore.
I don't want some trauma counselor to advise me to be soft,
to be open, to forgive my trespassers like all they stole from me
was some antique pocket watch.
I want to be reminded that Andromeda was not just
a king's daughter
but a galaxy all her own.
For the glacier that came along
and pushed the salt-ridden crust of my skin
into the Earth's mantle time after time
to slowly recede back into the sea from which it came
& melt into a mere puddle while I stand on the shores
feeling the tsunamis rise inside my chest.

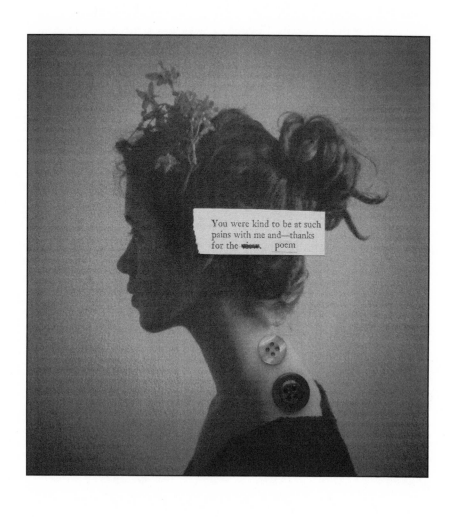

LETTERS TO MYSELF & EVERYONE ELSE

Letters to myself & everyone else. To survivors. Friends. People who don't understand. People who blame survivors. People who never try to understand or don't care to. Letters to attackers. To everyone who asked me if I asked for it. What I was wearing. How much I had to drink. Letters to myself reminding me those people are wrong. Letters to other survivors reminding them those people are wrong. To the people in a position of power who were supposed to keep me safe but did the opposite. To my attackers: you didn't ruin me.

TO MY BODY

Look, it's New Years and you're still alive. You used to have your breastbone replaced with a wishbone, both its ends tied to separate continents. I know you wanted the long end. I know you did. I know you wanted all your wishes to come true, or at the very least for someone to snap the string in two and pull your stretched-out cells back together. I know I hurt you, marked up your skin like graffiti, but he hurt you worse, and I want you to forgive yourself for that. When you heaved yourself out of our tremble-throated mother you almost kissed the man in the moon on his forehead with the wings you were born into. I know sometimes I clipped them shorter than you wanted. I know he tore them off altogether, and you will never get that back. I know that because of this, you will never become the astronaut you always envisioned yourself as. That you will never get your trip to Mars and the comets won't take you in as their child; NASA will never write you an acceptance letter disguised as a love poem. I know Orion's Belt is a noose of stars now instead of a lasso. But it won't always be this way— and I know I've lied to you before so why would you believe me now— but that is a promise and it's one I intend to keep.

TO A FRIEND WHO WENT BACK TO HIM

Do not cave like your grandmother's spine did
the day she fell down the stairs for the last time.
Loneliness is just a sheep in wolves' clothing.
You know exactly how to tame it, to let it eat out of your palm.
When he puts up his fists, remember that all palm lines start as maps
and eventually reincarnate into sorrow.
Once, his body led the way and taught you everything you knew—
now be your own teacher.
Relearn how to survive.
There will be days when the rain feels like his mouth on yours,
but know he is the thunderstorm
that once struck you down like lightning
and will no longer.
You have the courage to weather this.
Open your mouth and howl.
You are the coyote.
You, only you.
The moon will bow to you
just like he will
when you show up in his nightmares.

TO THE GIRLS WITH BROKEN HEARTS AND APOLOGETIC BODIES

Today, reclaim your apologies, all the times you spoke in class
without raising your hand first, the months
spent feeling like a black hole instead of the entire universe.
Take them back and raise them like your own, transform them into
the child you would have been if men had treated you
like a collection of neurons and constellations
rather than a ghost enveloped in skin.
Your voice will never be loud enough
until it reaches the rafters and collapses the whole house,
until the construction crew has to come by
and demolish the rest of what is left.
Speaking is never a crime, and your body has no right
to be fingerprinted
for a felony it never asked to pay for.
You have every right to throw way all the eggshells
you've spent lifetimes tiptoeing over.
Be the kind of woman who lives to the point of no return,
when I'm sorry turns to I'm sorry my reflection
is the opposite of what you're looking for,
and spread your wings so fast and hard
that the men who've pinned you to a corkboard
will never understand how you learned to fly.

TO WOMEN WHO ARE AFRAID OF THEIR BOYFRIENDS

He will teach you that getting away is like pulling teeth:
more and more painful until the job is done
and the sweet release of being disconnected finally hits.
You are worth more than the handprints on the ocean floor
you've left dozens of times when he pushed you back underwater
after months of tasting the sea air.
Even your blood loves you better than he ever could have
because even blood celebrates the fact that you're still alive.
When your grandfather taught you
the blinking you see in the night sky
is either an airplane or a shooting star, you always chose the plane
because at least planes can take you away
from somewhere you've never wanted to be.
Sometimes you can forget about the bruises
the same way some people forget the punctuation in their sentences
that give everything meaning.
But more often than not, you get stuck in this night
and he won't even let you have a glimpse of the stars.
So you dream about spaceships and launch pads
and how other planets get to exist in a universe
that won't hurt them.
And sometimes you wake up from a nightmare
wanting his arms around you
even though the only thing that caused the nightmare
was him.
But if Pluto can come back as a planet again, please know
one day you can be whoever you want to be too.
Without him.

DEAR "YOU KNOW WHO YOU ARE'S"

Go fuck yourselves.

Don't expect me to ask for signatures on the cast of this heartbreak
like pride is something you have any claim to.

The shadows of your egos are so large I wouldn't be surprised
if you tripped over them walking backwards.

There was no welcome mat set out before my body
when you kicked down the door.

Understand? It doesn't matter if you wiped your feet
before barging in. It doesn't matter if the lights were on.

It doesn't even matter if sometimes I invited you in.

Because when I said, *no, don't break the windows,*
you left the shattered panes inside
and didn't even bother to sweep them into the trash.

The lovechild of fear & anxiety is unlearning how to trust
and every day I have to keep feeding her and feeding her
because she's too weak to hold the spoon herself.

None of you will even pay alimony.

Go fuck yourselves
because no one will do it for you.

TO ALL THE WOMEN WHO SAID NO (IN MORE WAYS THAN WORDS)

Once your mother led you along window-shopping
in a town you never knew the name of.
Years later you are still window-shopping in mirrors to find yourself
after the long lines of men you never knew the names of.
Sometimes the old ghosts come back
and there's nothing more familiar
than your body trembling like a music note under someone else's
but just before you reach crescendo
you remember that all those years ago you said no.
You said no.
Please know:

> Your skin was not a yes.
> There is a fisherman's story of a young girl with seaweed hair
> and an oyster's pearl inside her belly.
> You, too, are made of light
> and the courage to fight tsunamis.
> Let love bless love under a big red moon.
> Every Monday and Sunday and every day in between
> it will never be your blame to keep.

Tonight, forget about the beginning.
End it and start another.
Let him hang his head in shame
while you hang your unnecessary guilt
on the umbrella hook of his back door.
Tomorrow it will rain.
He gets to face the storm he summoned
alone.

TO EVERYONE WHO WILL ROMANTICIZE PAIN LIKE THIS

Imagine having a séance with all your former selves
and never being able to apologize to them for the useless mistakes,
the crying over spilled milk,
the way you took their bodies for granted
and did not bother to clean up the bleeding you left them with.
Now imagine they all light candles of their own
and each one makes the same wish:
to never have met you.
That is what this pain is like.
It is the worst you could ever imagine.
Please think twice next time
before you speak of this
with bitterness on your tongue.

THE PIANO BURNER

Hey you. Yes, you. The one falling asleep in an ocean because it's easier than struggling to keep your head above water. There are so many directions. The compass rose, the wrong direction he took, is not your fault. It wasn't your hand twisting the needle; it was his and his only. I will love your blood until it sings again, until everything is a crescendo instead of a trembling silence. Hold that thought like psalms in your hands, beneath your breath and tongue where he won't ever find it. This is the hope that will keep you alive, will hide inside your bedroom desk drawers and stay preserved like dried flowers between dictionary pages.

I've seen you stub out your cigarettes in the halves of peaches. I've seen you do that to destroy something soft and beautiful just like you were. No, destruction isn't the right word for it. You were not destroyed. What was done to you was not a demolition. Got seas inside your belly still. Got bones like rafter beams. Your love still opens and closes like a door. He didn't take that out of you.

Honey you, yes you, are a grand piano that may have had the strings cut out, but it still remembers all the best melodies it used to play. And they will come alive again. You were not ended. You are not done. Play play play play play. It's time.

HUMMINGBIRD SONG (FOR A FRIEND & FELLOW SURVIVOR)

She is glass of water shaken by thundering footsteps,
voicebox strings snapped by greedy knife. She is hummingbird racing
away from the promise of being pinned to a corkboard.
He is the unseen bigfoot knocking over slumbering trees.
He pulls her legs apart without permission and calls it love;
she sees it for what it is.
If her dreams could be dissected like the cross section of a tree,
they would contain the word *No* repeated like a Buddhist chant
until he put his hand over her mouth and they grew muffled,
soft and crackly as autumn leaves underfoot.
She is trying to be the tough one. She is trying to hide
the bloodstained sheets under clean ones
that will end up stained too. She is drunk on feeling
like needing to apologize, drunk on self-blame.
He is pouring every bit of that blame down her throat
in a cheap red plastic cup until she grows waterlogged with it,
until every part of her body feels like a rotting tree.
But she is a brush fire, and she is burning, and she will not rest
until she sets him on fire too. She will turn him to cinders.
She will make every last flame count.
Then she will rise from the ashes like a phoenix
while he burns to the ground.

TO MYSELF

One day you will look back at this
and your heart will still have a migraine,
that soft place between your legs
will still ache, but faintly, like the pulse of a firefly.
There is no better glow than healing.
Memory will no longer be your enemy,
fear your best lover.
You gave all of yourself, and kept on giving and giving
until the stitches were at last ready to be undone.
The wound will sew itself.
Have patience.
The needle will find the thread.

ACKNOWLEDGMENTS

Great thanks to *Degenerates: Voices for Peace* for housing the poem, "Not All Men."

Several of the poems in this book have also been published on the author's personal writing blog, which can be found at:

www.writingsforwinter.tumblr.com

The author gratefully acknowledges her family, friends, loved ones, and Words Dance Publishing, who helped make this book possible.

Special thanks to MG, LR, AC, LB, CH, AB, and JR. You know who you are. Thank you a million times over.

Meggie Royer is a writer and photographer from the Midwest who is currently majoring in Psychology at Macalester College. Her poems have previously appeared in *Words Dance Magazine*, *The Harpoon Review*, *Melancholy Hyperbole*, and more. She has won national medals for her poetry and a writing portfolio in the Scholastic Art and Writing Awards, and was the Macalester Honorable Mention recipient of the 2015 Academy of American Poets Student Poetry Prize.

National Sexual Assault Hotline: A national crisis hotline operated by RAINN for the purpose of helping survivors of sexual violence. This hotline provides the caller with information about the closest rape crisis center. Hotline: 800-656-HOPE : *rainn.org/get-help/national-sexual-assault-hotline*

National Sexual Violence Resource Center: A large database of information pertaining to sexual violence, including legal information. : *nsvrc.org*

National Online Resource Center on Violence Against Women: A resource containing thousands of materials about violence against women and girls, focusing on intersections with other forms of oppression. : *vawnet.org*

GirlThrive: Girlthrive Inc. supports young women who have survived incest and other forms of sexual violence through thriverships, opportunities, and education. : *girlthrive.com*

Pandora's Aquarium: A rape, sexual assault, and sexual abuse survivor message board and chat room that performs as an online survivor support group. : *pandys.org/forums/index.php?act=idx*

RAINN: The rape, abuse, and incest national network, the nation's largest anti-sexual assault organization that includes phone & online hotlines, information about where to find crisis centers, international resources, and information about how to support loved ones who have experienced sexual violence. : *rainn.org*

The We Believe You Project: A Tumblr support blog for all survivors of the many forms of sexual violence. This blog includes advice, information about rape culture, and a series of YouTube episodes dedicated to debunking rape myths. It is also a place to share personal stories and receive support. : *webelieveyou.tumblr.com*

Self Care After Rape: A Tumblr blog run by survivors of sexual violence who provide advice and coping strategies to other survivors, and focuses on the long term healing journey. : *selfcareafterrape.tumblr.com*

Project Unbreakable: A photography project dedicated to giving a voice to survivors of sexual assault, domestic violence, and child abuse through art. : *projectunbreakable.tumblr.com*

Joyful Heart Foundation: Founded by Mariska Hargitay, this national organization with service hubs across the U.S. is aimed at carrying out their mission through healing, advocacy, and education. Joyful Heart also has several survivor programs, including wellness days and retreat programs. : *joyfulheartfoundation.org*

Other titles available from
WORDS DANCE PUBLISHING

CHLOE
Poetry by Kristina Haynes

| \$12 | 110 pages | 5.5" x 8.5" | softcover |

Chloe is brave and raw, adolescence mixed with salt. These poems are about how hungry we've been, how foolish, how lonely. Chloe is not quite girl nor woman, full of awkward bravery. Kristina is an electric voice that pulls Chloe apart page after page, her heartbreaks, her too many drinks, her romantic experiences of pleasure and pain. Chloe and Kristina make a perfect team to form an anthem for girls everywhere, an anthem that reassures us we deserve to take up space. Indeed, when I met Chloe, I too thought "This is the closest I've been to anybody in months."

— **MEGGIE ROYER**
Author of *Survival Songs*
and *Healing Old Wounds with New Stitches*

"Chloe is one of the most intimate books you'll read all year. Chloe is my new best friend. I want to eat burnt popcorn on her couch and watch Friends reruns. I want to borrow her clothing, write on her walls in lipstick. Chloe is not your dream girl. She doesn't have everything figured out. She's messy. She's always late. She promises old lovers she'll never call again. She teaches you what the word "indulgence" means. She's wonderful, wonderful, wonderful. In Chloe, Kristina Haynes digs into the grittiness of modern womanhood, of mothers and confusion and iPhones and two, maybe three-night-stands. Her truths are caramels on the tongue but are blunter, harsher on the way down. Kristina introduces us to a character I'll be thinking about for a very long time. Go read this book. Then write a poem. Then kiss someone. Then buy an expensive strain of tea and a new pillow. Then go read it again."

— **YASMIN BELKHYR**
Editor-in-Chief at *Winter Tangerine Review*

Other titles available from
WORDS DANCE PUBLISHING

LITERARY SEXTS
VOLUME 2

A Collection of Short & Sexy Love Poems

| $12 | 76 pages | 5.5" x 8.5" | softcover |

ISBN: 978-0692359594

This is the highly anticipated second volume of Literary Sexts! After over 1,000 copies of Literary Sexts Volume 1 being sold, we are super-excited to bring you a second volume! Literary Sexts is an annual modern day anthology of short love & sexy poems edited by Amanda Oaks & Caitlyn Siehl. These are poems that you would text to your lover. Poems that you would slip into a back pocket, suitcase, wallet or purse on the sly. Poems that you would write on slips of paper & stick under your crush's windshield wiper or pillow. Poems that you would write on a Post-it note & leave on the bathroom mirror. Poems that you would whisper into your lover's ear. Hovering around 40 contributors & 130 poems, this book reads is like one long & very intense conversation between two lovers. It's absolutely breathtaking.

This is for the leather
& the lace of you–

your flushed cheeks
& what set them ablaze.

Other titles available from
WORDS DANCE PUBLISHING

DOWRY MEAT
Poetry by Heather Knox

| \$12 | 110 pages | 5.5" x 8.5" | softcover |

Heather Knox's *Dowry Meat* is a gorgeous, tough-as-nails debut that arrives on your doorstep hungry and full of dark news. There's damage here, and obsession, and more haunted beauty in the wreckage of just about everything—relationships, apartment clutter, rough sex, the body, and of course the just-post apocalypse— than you or I could hope to find on our own. These are poems that remind us not that life is hard—that's old news—but that down there in the gravel and broken glass is where the truth-worth-hearing lies, and maybe the life worth living. If you were a city, Knox tells us, unflinching as always, *I'd... read your graffiti. Drink your tap water./Feel your smog and dirt stick to my sweat... If you were a city, I'd expect to be robbed.*

— JON LOOMIS
Author of *Vanitas Motel (winner of the FIELD prize)* and *The Pleasure Principle*

"Heather Knox's debut collection is a lyric wreath made of purulent ribbon and the most inviting of thorns. Tansy and tokophobia, lachrymosity and lavage are braided together in this double collection, which marries a sci-fi Western narrative to a lyric sequence. Both elapse in an impossible location made of opposites—futuristic nostalgia, or erotic displeasure—otherwise known as the universe in which we (attempt to) live."

— JOYELLE MCSWEENEY
Author of *The Necropastoral: Poetry, Media, Occults & Salamandrine: 8 Gothics*

"*Dowry Meat*'s apocalyptic fever dream myth-making bleeds into what we might call the poetry of witness or the tradition of the confessional, except that these lines throb with lived experience and a body isn't necessarily a confession. Heather Knox's poems are beautifully wrought and beautifully raw."

— DORA MALECH
Author of *Shore Ordered Ocean & Say So*

Other titles available from
WORDS DANCE PUBLISHING

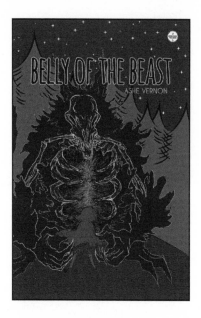

BELLY OF THE BEAST
Poetry by Ashe Vernon

| \$12 | 82 pages | 5.5" x 8.5" | softcover |
ISBN: 978-0692300541

"Into the Belly of the Beast we crawl with Ashe as our guide; into the dark visceral spaces where love, lust, descent and desire work their transformative magic and we find ourselves utterly altered in the reading. A truly gifted poet and truth-spiller, Ashe's metaphors create images within images, leading us to question the subjective truths, both shared and hidden, in personal relationship – to the other, and to oneself. Unflinching in her approach, her poetry gives voice to that which most struggle to admit – even if only to themselves. And as such, Belly of the Beast is a work of startling courage and rich depth – a darkly delicious pleasure."

— AMY PALKO
Goddess Guide, Digital Priestess & Writer

"It isn't often you find a book of poetry that is as unapologetic, as violent, as moving as this one. Ashe's writing is intense and visceral. You feel the punch in your gut while you're reading, but you don't question it. You know why it's there and you almost welcome it."

— CAITLYN SIEHL
Author of *What We Buried*

"The poems you are about to encounter are the fierce time capsules of girl-hood, girded with sharp elbows, surprise kisses, the meanders of wander-lust. We need voices this strong, this true for the singing reminds us that we are not alone, that someone, somewhere is listening for the faint pulse that is our wish to be seen. Grab hold, this voice will be with us forever."

— RA WASHINGTON
GuidetoKulchurCleveland.com

Other titles available from
WORDS DANCE PUBLISHING

POEM YOUR HEART OUT
Prompts, Poems & Room to Add Your Own
Volume 1

| $15 | 158 pages | 5.5" x 8.5" | softcover |

ISBN: 978-0692317464

PROMPT BOOK • ANTHOLOGY • WORKBOOK

Words Dance Publishing teamed up with the Writer's Digest's Poetic Asides blog to make their Poem-A-Day challenge this year even more spectacular!

Part poetry prompt book, part anthology of the best poems written during the 2014 April PAD (Poem-A-Day) Challenge on the Poetic Asides blog (by way of Writer's Digest) & part workbook, let both, the prompt & poem, inspire you to create your own poetic masterpieces. Maybe you participated in April & want to document your efforts during the month. Maybe you're starting now, like so many before you, with just a prompt, an example poem, & an invitation to poem your heart out! You're encouraged—heck, dared—to write your own poems inside of this book!

This book is sectioned off by Days, each section will hold the prompt for that day, the winning poem for that day & space for you to place the poem you wrote for that day's prompt inside.

Just a few of the guest judges: Amy King, Bob Hicok, Jericho Brown, Nate Pritts, Kristina Marie Darling & Nin Andrews...

Challenge yourself, your friend, a writing workshop or your class to this 30 Day Poem-A-Day Challenge!

THIS IS AN INVITATION TO POEM YOUR HEART OUT!

Other titles available from
WORDS DANCE PUBLISHING

I EAT CROW + BLUE COLLAR AT BEST
Poetry by Amanda Oaks + Zach Fishel

| $15 | 124 pages | 5.5" x 8.5" | softcover |

Home is where the heart is and both poets' hearts were raised in the Appalachian region of Western Pennsylvania surrounded by coal mines, sawmills, two-bit hotel taverns, farms, churches and cemeteries. These poems take that region by the throat and shake it until it's bloody and then, they breathe it back to life. This book is where you go when you're looking for nostalgia to kick you in the teeth. This is where you go when you're 200 miles away from a town you thought you'd never want to return to but suddenly you're pining for it.

Amanda and Zach grew up 30 miles from each other and met as adults through poetry. Explore both the male and female perspective of what it's like to grow up hemmed in by an area's economic struggle. These poems mine through life, love, longing and death, they're for home and away, and the inner strength that is not deterred by any of those things.

SPLIT BOOK #1

What are Split Books?

Two full-length books from two poets in one + there's a collaborative split between the poets in the middle!

COLLECT THEM ALL!

Other titles available from
WORDS DANCE PUBLISHING

SHAKING THE TREES
Poetry by Azra Tabassum

| \$12 | 72 pages | 5.5" x 8.5" | softcover |

ISBN: 978-0692232408

From the very first page *Shaking the Trees* meets you at the edge of the forest, extends a limb & seduces you into taking a walk through the dark & light of connection. Suddenly, like a gunshot in the very-near distance, you find yourself traipsing though a full-blown love story that you can't find your way out of because the story is actually the landscape underneath your feet. It's okay though, you won't get lost— you won't go hungry. Azra shakes every tree along the way so their fruit blankets the ground before you. She picks up pieces & hands them to you but not before she shows you how she can love you so gently it will feel like she's unpeeling you carefully from yourself. She tells you that it isn't about the bite but the warm juice that slips from the lips down chin. She holds your hand when you're trudging through the messier parts, shoes getting stuck in the muck of it all, but you'll keep going with the pulp of the fruit still stuck in-between your teeth, the juice will dry in the crooks of your elbows & in the lines on your palms. You'll taste bittersweet for days.

"I honestly haven't read a collection like this before, or at least I can't remember having read one. My heart was wrecked by Azra. It's like that opening line in Fahrenheit 451 when Bradbury says, "It was a pleasure to burn." It really was a pleasure being wrecked by it."

— **NOURA**
of *NouraReads*

"I wanted to cry and cheer and fuck. I wanted to take the next person I saw and kiss them straight on the lips and say, "Remember this moment for the rest of your life."

— **CHELSEA MILLER**

SPARKLEFAT

Poetry by Melissa May

| $12 | 62 pages | 5.5" x 8.5" | softcover |

SparkleFat is a loud, unapologetic, intentional book of poetry about my body, about your body, about fat bodies and how they move through the world in every bit of their flash and spark and burst. Some of the poems are painful, some are raucous celebrations, some are reminders and love letters and quiet gifts back to the vessel that has traveled me so gracefully - some are a hymnal of yes, but all of them sparkle. All of them don't mind if you look – really. They built their own house of intention, and they draped that shit in lime green sequins. All of them intend to be seen. All of them have no more fucks to give about a world that wants them to be quiet.

"I didn't know how much I needed this book until I found myself, three pages in, ugly crying on the plane next to a concerned looking business man. This book is the most glorious, glittery pink permission slip. It made me want to go on a scavenger hunt for every speck of shame in my body and sing hot, sweaty R&B songs to it. There is no voice more authentic, generous and resounding than Melissa May. From her writing, to her performance, to her role in the community she delivers fierce integrity & staggering passion. From the first time I watched her nervously step to the mic, to the last time she crushed me in a slam, it is has been an honor to watch her astound the poetry slam world and inspire us all to be not just better writers but better people. We need her."

— **LAUREN ZUNIGA**
Author of *The Smell of Good Mud*

"*SparkleFat* is a firework display of un-shame. Melissa May's work celebrates all of the things we have been so long told deserved no streamers. This collection invites every fat body out to the dance and steams up the windows in the backseat of the car afterwards by kissing the spots we thought (or even hoped) no one noticed but are deserving of love just the same as our mouths."

— **RACHEL WILEY**
Author of *Fat Girl Finishing School*

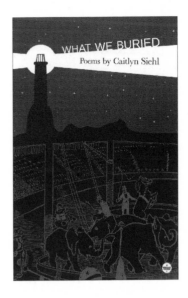

WHAT WE BURIED
Poetry by Caitlyn Siehl

| $12 | 64 pages | 5.5" x 8.5" | softcover |

ISBN: 978-0615985862

This book is a cemetery of truths buried alive. The light draws you in where you will find Caitlyn there digging. When you get close enough, she'll lean in & whisper, Baby, buried things will surface no matter what, get to them before they get to you first. Her unbounded love will propel you to pick up a shovel & help— even though the only thing you want to do is kiss her lips, kiss her hands, kiss every one of her stretch marks & the fire that is raging in pit of her stomach. She'll see your eyes made of devour & sadness, she'll hug you & say, Baby, if you eat me alive, I will cut my way out of your stomach. Don't let this be your funeral. Teach yourself to navigate the wound.

"It takes a true poet to write of love and desire in a way that manages to surprise and excite. Caitlyn Siehl does this in poem after poem and makes it seem effortless. Her work shines with a richness of language and basks in images that continue to delight and astound with multiple readings. What We Buried is a treasure from cover to cover."

— **WILLIAM TAYLOR JR.**
Author of *An Age of Monsters*

Other titles available from
WORDS DANCE PUBLISHING

LITERARY SEXTS

A Collection of Short & Sexy Love Poems
(Volume 1)

| $12 | 42 pages | 5.5" x 8.5" | softcover |

ISBN: 978-0615959726

Literary Sexts is a modern day anthology of short love poems with subtle erotic undertones edited by Amanda Oaks & Caitlyn Siehl. Hovering around 50 contributors & 124 poems, this book reads is like one long & very intense conversation between two lovers. It's absolutely breathtaking. These are poems that you would text to your lover. Poems that you would slip into a back pocket, suitcase, wallet or purse on the sly. Poems that you would write on slips of paper & stick under your crush's windshield wiper. Poems that you would write on a Post-it note & leave on the bathroom mirror.

HIT #1
ON AMAZON'S
HOT NEW
RELEASE LIST!

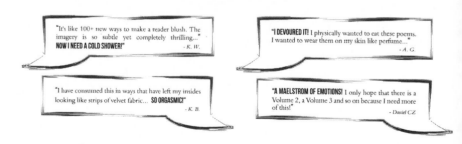

"It's like 100+ new ways to make a reader blush. The imagery is so subtle yet completely thrilling..." **NOW I NEED A COLD SHOWER!"**   - K. W.

"**I DEVOURED IT!** I physically wanted to eat these poems. I wanted to wear them on my skin like perfume..."   - A. G.

"I have consumed this in ways that have left my insides looking like strips of velvet fabric... **SO ORGASMIC!"**   - K. B.

"**A MAELSTROM OF EMOTIONS!** I only hope that there is a Volume 2, a Volume 3 and so on because I need more of this!"   - Daniel CZ

Other titles available from
WORDS DANCE PUBLISHING

LOVE AND OTHER SMALL WARS

Poetry by Donna-Marie Riley

| \$12 | 76 pages | 5.5" x 8.5" | softcover |

ISBN: 978-0615931111

Love and Other Small Wars reminds us that when you come back from combat usually the most fatal of wounds are not visible. Riley's debut collection is an arsenal of deeply personal poems that embody an intensity that is truly impressive yet their hands are tender. She enlists you. She gives you camouflage & a pair of boots so you can stay the course through the minefield of her heart. You will track the lovely flow of her soft yet fierce voice through a jungle of powerful imagery on womanhood, relationships, family, grief, sexuality & love, amidst other matters. Battles with the heart aren't easily won but Riley hits every mark. You'll be relieved that you're on the same side. Much like war, you'll come back from this book changed.

"Riley's work is wise, intense, affecting, and uniquely crafted. This collection illuminates her ability to write with both a gentle hand and a bold spirit. She inspires her readers and creates an indelible need inside of them to consume more of her exceptional poetry. I could read *Love and Other Small Wars* all day long…and I did."

— **APRIL MICHELLE BRATTEN**
editor of *Up the Staircase Quarterly*

"Riley's poems are personal, lyrical and so vibrant they practically leap off the page, which also makes them terrifying at times. A beautiful debut."

— **BIANCA STEWART**

Tammy Foster Brewer is the type of poet who makes me wish I could write poetry instead of novels. From motherhood to love to work, Tammy's poems highlight the extraordinary in the ordinary and leave the reader wondering how he did not notice what was underneath all along. I first heard Tammy read 'The Problem is with Semantics' months ago, and it's stayed with me ever since. Now that I've read the entire collection, I only hope I can make room to keep every one of her poems in my heart and mind tomorrow and beyond.

— **NICOLE ROSS**, author

NO GLASS ALLOWED
Poetry by Tammy Foster Brewer

$12 | 56 pages | 6" x 9" | softcover | ISBN: 978-0615870007

Brewer's collection is filled with uncanny details that readers will wear like the accessories of womanhood. Fishing the Chattahoochee, sideways trees, pollen on a car, white dresses and breast milk, and so much more -- all parts of a deeply intellectual pondering of what is often painful and human regarding the other halves of mothers and daughters, husbands and wives, lovers and lost lovers, children and parents.

— **NICHOLAS BELARDES**
author of *Songs of the Glue Machines*

Tammy deftly juxtaposes distinct imagery with stories that seem to collide in her brilliant poetic mind. Stories of transmissions and trees and the words we utter, or don't. Of floods and forgiveness, conversations and car lanes, bread and beginnings, awe and expectations, desire and leaps of faith that leave one breathless, and renewed.

"When I say I am a poet / I mean my house has many windows" has to be one of the best descriptions of what it's like to be a contemporary female poet who not only holds down a day job and raises a family, but whose mind and heart regularly file away fleeting images and ideas that might later be woven into something permanent, and perhaps even beautiful. This ability is not easily acquired. It takes effort, and time, and the type of determination only some writers, like Tammy, possess and are willing to actively exercise.

— **KAREN DEGROOT CARTER**
author of *One Sister's Song*

Other titles available from
WORDS DANCE PUBLISHING

Unrequited love? We've all been there.

Enter:

WHAT TO DO AFTER SHE SAYS NO
by Kris Ryan.

This skillfully designed 10-part poem explores what it's like to ache for someone. This is the book you buy yourself or a friend when you are going through a breakup or a one-sided crush, it's the perfect balance between aha, humor & heartbreak.

WHAT TO DO AFTER SHE SAYS NO
A Poem by Kris Ryan

$10 | 104 pages | 5" x 8" | softcover | ISBN: 978-0615870045

"*What to Do After She Says No* takes us from Shanghai to the interior of a refrigerator, but mostly dwells inside the injured human heart, exploring the aftermath of emotional betrayal. This poem is a compact blast of brutality, with such instructions as "Climb onto the roof and jump off. If you break your leg, you are awake. If you land without injury, pinch and twist at your arm until you wake up." Ryan's use of the imperative often leads us to a reality where pain is the only outcome, but this piece is not without tenderness, and certainly not without play, with sounds and images ricocheting off each other throughout. Anticipate the poetry you wish you knew about during your last bad breakup; this poem offers a first "foothold to climb out" from that universal experience."

— **LISA MANGINI**

"Reading Kris Ryan's *What To Do After She Says No* is like watching your heart pound outside of your chest. Both an unsettling visual experience and a hurricane of sadness and rebirth—this book demands more than just your attention, it takes a little bit of your soul, and in the end, makes everything feel whole again."

— **JOHN DORSEY**
author of ***Tombstone Factory***

"*What to Do After She Says No* is exquisite. Truly, perfectly exquisite. It pulls you in on a familiar and wild ride of a heart blown open and a mind twisting in an effort to figure it all out. It's raw and vibrant...and in the same breath comforting. I want to crawl inside this book and live in a world where heartache is expressed so magnificently.

— **JO ANNA ROTHMAN**
MA, Coach & Conjurer of Electric Creative Wholeness

WORDS DANCE PUBLISHING has one aim:

To spread mind-blowing / heart-opening poetry.

Words Dance artfully & carefully wrangles words that were born to dance wildly in the heart-mind matrix. Rich, edgy, raw, emotionally-charged energy balled up & waiting to whip your eyes wild; we rally together words that were written to make your heart go boom right before they slay your mind.

Words Dance Publishing is an independent press out of Pennsylvania. We work closely & collaboratively with all of our writers to ensure that their words continue to breathe in a sound & stunning home. Most importantly though, we leave the windows in these homes unlocked so you, the reader, can crawl in & throw one fuck of a house party.

To learn more about our books, authors, events & Words Dance Poetry Magazine, visit:

WORDSDANCE.COM

DO YOU WRITE POETRY?
Submit it to our biweekly online magazine!

We publish poems every Tuesday & Thursday on website.

Come see what all the fuss is about!

We like Poems that sneak up on you. Poems that make out with you. Poems that bloody your mouth just to kiss it clean. Poems that bite your cheek so you spend all day tonguing the wound. Poems that vandalize your heart. Poems that act like a tin can phone connecting you to your childhood. Fire Alarm Poems. Glitterbomb Poems. Jailbreak Poems. Poems that could marry the land or the sea; that are both the hero & the villain. Poems that are the matches when there is a city-wide power outage. Poems that throw you overboard just dive in & save your ass. Poems that push you down on the stoop in front of history's door screaming at you to knock. Poems that are soft enough to fall asleep on. Poems that will still be clinging to the walls inside of your bones on your 90th birthday. We like poems. Submit yours.

WORDSDANCE.COM

WORDS DANCE
PUBLISHING

12757917R00086

Printed in Poland
by Amazon Fulfillment
Poland Sp. z o.o., Wrocław